The Morecambe & Wise Special

BY ERIC & ERNIE

WHAT THE CRITICS SAID:

'Eric and Ernie write for the whole Family'
The Godfather

'We'll never let them go'
BBC

'A soul-searching drama of human life and achievement'
The Times (possibly about another book)

A STAR BOOK
published by
the Paperback Division of
W.H. ALLEN & Co. Ltd.

At home, my husband

and we, with closest friends.

ACKNOWLEDGMENTS

We would like to thank Harold Pinter and Alexander Solzhenitsyn
for their kind and generous comments but we can't because they didn't make any.

Thanks are due to James Herriot for vetting the entire manuscript and a
very special debt is owed to the Inland Revenue. Also to Valerie Singleton, the
Consumers' Friend, for her seal of approval (we'd like to thank you in person
sometime Valerie) and to Mary Whitehouse for the only dirty joke in the book.

We are grateful to the Chinese Army for the crowd scenes, to the
National Gallery for certain pictures (they don't know about those yet) and to
the English language for throwing up great writers like what we are.

Morecambe *Lancs* [Mawr Cum, "great hollow"]. Mun. bor. and watering place. Ecclesiastical district no 3834. Mild and equable. There are some remarkable stone coffins to be seen. In Morecambe Bay, at 12 fathoms, is Morecambe Bay Light Vessel, with group flashing.

(From Bartholomew's Gazetteer of the British Isles)

Wise [*wiz*] *n* having or showing wisdom; perceptive, prudent, discreet; well informed; (*sl*) knowing all about, Well warned against, w. guy (*sl*) one who thinks himself cleverer than he is.

(From The Penguin English Dictionary)

INTRODUCTION
by Des O'Connor

The famous Eric Morecambe and Ernie Wise O.B.E.s
need no Introduction.
So here instead is a picture of me.

Postbag

APPLICATION FOR APPEARANCE IN AN ERN EPIC

(Block letters please)
Please answer the following questions truthfully.

SURNAME MOORE
FORENAMES PATRICK *(TALKING VERY VERY VERY VERY VERY FAST)*
OCCUPATION
ADDRESS A BLACK HOLE *(WITH WIFE & 2 QUARKS)*
SEX APPEAL NEBULOUS
FAVOURITE BREAKFAST FOOD ASTRONOMIC MARS
FEE PROPOSED
ENCLOSED DOWN-PAYMENT MY TAILOR (ANONYMOUS) PAYABLE TO JODRELL BANK
I WISH TO APPEAR IN: STARS ON SUNDAY
2nd. Choice A NEW SUIT

(To be signed by applicant)

APPLICATION FOR APPEARANCE IN AN ERN EPIC

(Block letters please)
Please answer the following questions truthfully.

SURNAME WEDGWOOD BENN
FORENAMES COMRADE
ADDRESS NUMBER 10 (SOON)
OCCUPATION NUMBER 10 (SOON)
SEX APPEAL COLLECTIVE
FAVOURITE BREAKFAST FOOD CHICKEN (RIGHT WING ONLY)
FEE PROPOSED CARRIED
PAYABLE TO MY SHOP (CLOSED)
ENCLOSED DOWN-PAYMENT ONE KITCHEN CABINET
I WISH TO APPEAR IN:
1st. Choice LUCKY JIM
2nd. Choice NUMBER 10 (SO...

APPLICATION FOR APPEARANCE ...

(Block letters please)
Please answer the following quest...

SURNAME VI
ADDRESS HALO!
SEX APPEAL INFALL...
FAVOURITE BREAKFAST FOO...
PROPOSED MASSES
DOWN-PAYMENT
TO APPEAR IN:
...ce THE ITALIAN JOB
2nd.

(...WRITE IN THIS SPACE ...ERIC'S USE ONLY)

APPLICATION F... APPEARANCE L...

(Block letters please)
Please answer the following questions tru...

SURNAME RICHMOND
ADDRESS NEVER WORN ONE
SEX APPEAL PLEASE G...
FAVOURITE BREAKFAST FOOD
FEE PROPOSED I'D GIVE EVERYTHING
ENCLOSED DOWN-PAYMENT S...
I WISH TO APPEAR IN:
1st. Choice NUDE WITH VIOLIN
2nd.

DO NOT WRITE IN THIS SPACE
(FOR ERIC'S USE ONLY)

APPLICATION FOR APPEARANCE IN AN ERN EPIC

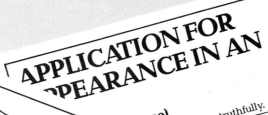

(Block letters please)
Please answer the following questions truthfully.

SURNAME MAGNUSSON   FORENAMES MANGUS MONGOOSE MAGNUS

ADDRESS DIGS   OCCUPATION PYRAMID SELLING

SEX APPEAL PASSABLE

FAVOURITE BREAKFAST FOOD BRAINS

FEE PROPOSED ANYTHING QUESTIONABLE   PAYABLE TO THE BANKS OF THE NILE

ENCLOSED DOWN-PAYMENT PASS

I WISH TO APPEAR IN:
1st. Choice OPPORTUNITY KNOCKS   2nd. Choice (BOTH PARTS PLEASE) THE INTELLIGENCE MEN

Mag Magnusson
(To be signed by applicant)

DO NOT WRITE IN THIS SPACE
(FOR ERIC'S USE ONLY)

APPLICATION FOR APPEARANCE IN AN ERN EPIC

FORENAMES ALEXANDER "POPE"

OCCUPATION MONTINI PEOPLE

QUAKERS

...LE TO ALEXANDER VI

...OH CALCUTTA!

ERN EPIC

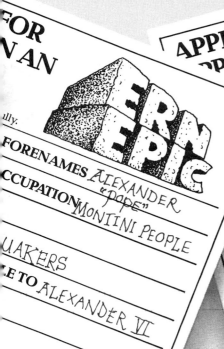

...RENAMES FIONA (NÉE VIRGINIA)

...CUPATION MEN ONLY

...GENEROUSLY

...ME LAID (HA! HA!)

...LE TO MEN ONLY

...G TO YOU!

...ce NUDE WITHOUT VIOLIN

APPLICATION FOR APPEARANCE IN AN ERN EPIC

(Block letters please)
Please answer the following questions truthfully.

SURNAME NIXON   FORENAMES RICHARD MILLSTONE

ADDRESS PRESIDENTIAL   OCCUPATION RECORDER

SEX APPEAL NONE WHATSOEVER

FAVOURITE BREAKFAST FOOD SOUR GRAPES

FEE PROPOSED PARDON?   PAYABLE TO ALL THE PRESIDENT'S MEN

ENCLOSED DOWN-PAYMENT ~~~~

I WISH TO APPEAR IN:
1st. Choice THE PARDONER'S TALE   2nd. Choice SPOOL FOR SCANDAL or PLANET OF THE TAPES

R Nixon

DO NOT WRITE IN THIS SPACE
(FOR ERIC'S USE ONLY)

Bishop Odour Morecambe
(999-1077)

known as "The Warrior Priest"
and "The Pope's friend" who
failed to turn up for the Battle of
Hastings due to a traffic jam on
the A21. He coined the phrase
"That's one in the eye for Harold."

Sir Jasper 'Needles' Morecambe
(1300-?)

Minister of Health during the
Black Death who lived a very
long time.

Sir Christopher Morecambe
(1600-1700)

who started the Great Fire of
London and earned fame and
fortune for rebuilding it.

The House of Morecambe

Sir Jack 'I'm all Right' Morecambe
(1750-1830)

who fought for Napoleon and
Wellington at Waterloo, in that
order.

Sir Walter Morecambe
(1550-1660)

courtier and seadog who used
Queen Elizabeth's cloak to keep
his feet dry in the mud.

Lord Pullover 'Daredevil' Morecambe
(1800-1900)

who transferred to the Heavy
Brigade during a well-known
cavalry charge at Balaclava.

Eric Morcum
by
ERNEST WISE O.B.E.

When they asked me a couple of minutes ago to write something about Eric, my home help, I said, 'Where's the money?' You see, I do have to keep up this facade of being mean and tight-fisted which has been built up over the years by Eric. Really, I'm kind and gentle and occasionally quite generous with my time, but I do feel that great talent –like what I've got–should not go unrewarded–so where's the money? But we were talking about four-eyes. Well, I first met Eric on the train at Crewe. All great double acts start at Crewe. He was eating his ticket at the time. I discovered afterwards he was nibbling out the date before the collector came. I said to him, 'Why don't we do a double act together? Do you know a little joke?' He said, 'Yes, you.' And that's how it all started...he's been insulting me ever since. Of course I handle the money! We split everything straight down the middle, 60-40. I explained to him I get the 60, but I do have to pay more tax than him.

Somebody once asked me the definition of comic relief. I said when Eric goes home. I first saw Eric give his audition for Jack Hylton in Manchester. He was wearing a black beret, boot-lace tie, cut down dress suit held together with a large safety pin, red socks and holding a large lollipop. I thought, how anybody can walk about in the street dressed like that is ridiculous.

He sang a song called *I'm not all There*, then did his impression of Flanagan and Allen but only did Allen; I've never been able to work that one out. My valet brought him to my dressing room, number one. (Jack Hylton always changed with the band.) Eric said Good God. I said yes. He said, 'I never thought I would be given a private audience with such a great man.' I said, 'Not many people do. Get up off your knees.'

That's how we met. Now my personal opinion of Eric. I've always found him a shy, sensitive person, not one for pushing himself forward. Rather like a liberal–lonely, but with his feet planted firmly in the air. Very good to his Mother; never goes home. Doesn't really need glasses, quite capable of drinking straight out of the bottle. Always respectful to me, he knows his

Inquiring

pensive

vital

place and calls me his little fat friend who wears a wig. He says you can't see the join, that I have short fat hairy legs, and am mean with my money. He cracks jokes like 'He's got moths in his wallet that have not learned to fly yet; he's got short arms and long pockets; he suffers from rheumatism in the right hip from stealing wet change off the bar.' He says I collect white fivers; drink very quickly because I had one knocked over once; calls me little Ern-get the tea ern. Says I'm dynamite with the girls but I've only got a short fuse.

I would like to defend myself. First of all money is not everything-there are stocks and shares and travellers checks. We have never let money come between us. It never gets past me. I don't wear a wig; it's Eric who is going bald. At least baldness has one advantage when you have visitors, you only have to straighten your tie. I said to him the other day, 'You're going bald.' He said, 'When you are losing your hair at the front it means you're a great thinker and when you're losing it at the back it means you're a great lover.' I said, 'But yours is going at the front and the back.' He said, 'Yes I think I'm a great lover.'

The only fault I can find is that Eric is an egotist; he's more interested in himself than me. But he's the bravest man I know. He actually finished a meal in a motorway cafe. I think one of my biggest regrets in all the years I've been in the theatre is that I've never been able to sit in the audience and watch me. Eric looks like an identikit picture of Shaw Taylor. And I'd still like to know what he does for a living.

Egbert Wise
(750-806)

playwright, author of the well-known Anglo Saxon musical comedy *Make Me an Offa*.

Lady Godawful Wise
(1040-1080)

playwright, who rode naked to the Coventry Hippodrome for her play *Much Ado about Very Little*.

William 'Shakespeare' Wise
(1564-1616)

copywriter, who copied the writings of his contemporaries under his own name. He lived uninvited with the Royal Family and was known to his bank manager as Merry Wise of Windsor.

The house of Wise

Oscar Wise
(1856-1900)

playwright, whose works include
The Importance of Being Earnest
and *Look Back in Earnest.*

Edward 'Gibbon' Wise
(1737-1794)

whose multi-volume saga of
Italian cricket, *Decline and Fall
of the Roman Umpire,* sold no
copies at all.

Sir Charles Wise
(1812-1870)

author of *David Diamondfield,
Nicholas Silverby* and a *Tale of
Two Banks.*

Eric Wise by Eric Morecambe, — I mean Ernie Wild by… I'll start again.

My little Fat Friend

by the Tall Goodlooking One with the Glasses.

What can I say about Ernie Wise that has not already been said…Very little…And that's been said a few times…

Youm, the people whom have been foolhardy enough to steal this book from your local bookstore only see Eddie Wise as a character flitting on your TV screens. A rather gay little being…whose looks of distrust–his quick nervous giggles and his long-suffering pauses usually mean he's forgotten what comes next. A man whose great performing ability is sometimes marred by the fact that I've tightened the belt on his special appliance a couple of notches…

To us whom are within the portals of showbizz, Ernie Wise is a living legend...he is loved...and envied. Who has been more honoured?

O.B.E.
Freedom of the city of London
Seven S.F.T.A. awards
Two awards by the Sun newspaper
Two awards by Radio Enterprises
Two awards by the Variety Club of Great Britain
One award by the Grand Order of the Water Rats
One special award from the Grand Order of the Water Rats
Six Command Performances
Two special Command Performances at Windsor Castle

You put all these things together and what have you got...I'll tell you what you've got...a crawler...that's what you've got... How many people know that Ernie White is a great Wreckontour. Also a great gourmet...oh yes, he knows all there is to know about wines... I have actually been with him when we've been dining out with some of the Beautiful People of the Jet Lag Set...and many's the time I've heard him say to the headwaiter, 'I'll leave it to you, sunbeam!'

A man about women.

A sure sign of a man about women... Do you realize that he is one of the few men whom can actually tell the difference between a Welsh Rarebit and a Scotch Egg by touch alone... The man has a natural bent which I can verify as I have kept the negatives...

But what you want to know–and rightly so–is what is Bernie White like off the screen...is there another Ernie Wine? Well! Only I can tell you...because I know Ernie Wyse almost as well as his bank manager in Peterborough. First of all he's good to his mother as he never goes home.

Good to his mother

Who was it who said Ernie Wise is a myth?... Me...it was me who said that...I said it while I was drunk–I meant to say miss.

How many of you people watching this page know anything about his war record?... Probably about two, and one of those had a small black moustache and a stiff arm... During the First World War our little hero had two horses and a nurse shot from under him... And on the day that the Second World War was declared...do you know what he was doing like the great man he is?... He was at his local saw-mill thinking about cutting his finger off... But he went into Espionage–He thought it was a shop at the back of Swan and Edgar's–

Living legend.

In 1940 he blew up four trains and two ammunition dumps...so then they sent him overseas. After that he came home to his beloved England...and went into Banking and Showbizz. He came into money through a lucky stroke... His rich uncle had one and left him everything...

Rich, young, virile.

In short (and he is) I quote from his contemporaries.

Sir Glenda Jackson
'I'd like him for my key-ring'

Mary Wilson
'I don't know whether he's bald or not, as I've never seen him without his wig'

Andre Previn
'Good God'–and–'Never again'

Robert Morley
'He says he's a self-made man ... and I think it's rather sweet of him to take the blame'

Gayle Hunnicut
'Once we went out for dinner together ... I picked up the bill and he picked up the tip'

Susan Hampshire
'Same as Andre Previn'

The Man In The Street
'Well...eesacreempuffinee'

Lord Olivier
'Mr Wise's writing is riveting, and that's what he should be doing ... not writing, but in a Dock Yard riveting'

Note: Lord Olivier's quote was taken while he was under the influence of a truth serum

1 'Horrifying'–
Des O'Connor

2 'I cannot think of a
finer man'–
Lew Grade

3 'I cannot fault this
book'–
Ronnie Corbett

I·SPY
LEW GRADE
BOOK

Small
is
beautiful

with Tripleday

The
AA
Guide to
Harpenden

6 'Pure
plagiarism'
–R.A.C.

PoleVaulting
made difficult

by Eric Morecambe

7 'Should do
wonders for
the profession'–
Royal
College of
Surgeons

10 'A welcome piece of
grovelling'–
Ian Trethowan

The Magnificent
BBC

A sincere tribute to the clever,
generous, kind, good contracts
department from a grateful
Eric and Ernie

**How to
Dance**
Eric Morecambe & Ernie Wise
& Rudolf Nureyev

GREAT PLAYS
I have wrote

ERNIE WISE

11 'My lawyers are
investigating'–
Rudolf Nureyev

12 'Don't call us, we'll
call You'–
Laurence Olivier

13 'Pure fantasy'–
King Kong,
Sunday Times

**A Message from
Ernie Wise:**
*'From the anals of
literature we bring you
the cultural
foundations which
comprise the essence
of our civilization so
that your own mind
can flower like what
mine does with the
great thoughts of the
past present and
future'*

**A Message from
Eric Morecambe:**
'Buy them'

**A Message from
Antonia Fraser:**
*'Obviously no one
in their right mind...'*

The Wise Book Club

4 'I did it differently'
Ezra Pound

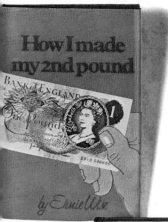

How I made my 2nd pound
by Ernie Wise

5 'Horrifying'–
Eric Morecambe

Guide to Des O'Connor

9 'A fine work from a master of the English language'–Arthur Mullard

8 'Great'–
Ernie Wise

V.I.P.
The Autobiography of Ernie Wise

The Concise
English Dictionarry

Words by
Ernest Wise OBE

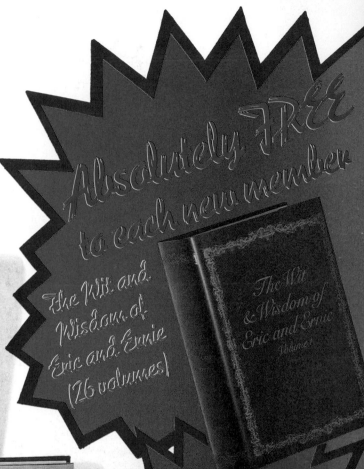

Absolutely FREE to each new member

The Wit and Wisdom of Eric and Ernie (26 volumes)

The Wit & Wisdom of Eric and Ernie Volume 1

and

The Complete Des O'Connor Joke Leaflet

My Hairy Friends by Eric Morecambe

Keep Fit with Eric

A Scrapbook of Cheque Stubs by Ernie Wise

14 'A simple tale of his legs; short and moving'–
Sunday Times

15 'The lads nearly died of fright'–Don Revie

16 'An indispensable record of Ernie's chequered career'–Inland Revenue

Send No Money Now Just post this coupon tomorrow with your cheque for the price of **Just Twenty Books** And then select **ONE BOOK** per day which will arrive together with our representative to **Save you Posting** your money because he will take it from you. In this way you will build a **Magnificent Library** of **Thousands of Copies** of the same book.

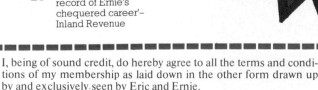

I, being of sound credit, do hereby agree to all the terms and conditions of my membership as laid down in the other form drawn up by and exclusively seen by Eric and Ernie.
If not **COMPLETELY SATISFIED** I agree not to terminate my membership.

Name..

Address..

Annual Income ....

Instant Wisdom is yours.

Just present your WISECARD at any establishment and see them <u>grovel</u>.

some advantages of WISECARD:
- **Have people <u>queueing</u> for advice.**
- **Make Magnus Magnusson look <u>stupid</u>.**
- **Walk into <u>any</u> University.**
- **Know <u>everything</u> there is to know.**
- **Spend 5 minutes in Claridges.**

If you apply within 1 hour you will receive a free pair of "Clever" specs to start you off on your knowledge & Wisdom trip.

To receive a WISECARD you must answer the following questions correctly:

NAME _____

ADDRESS _____

Enough is not enough!
You need MORE!

Eleven fabulous girls around the world have agreed to

Welcome this Card

If you are lucky enough to find one of these

Show her your Morecard. SHE WILL

Take you to her place to meet mother!

Teach you French cooking!!

Introduce you to her husband!!!

Take off Mike Yarwood!!!!

Do the dance of the seven dwarfs!

Just send £10 together with your

Own Girlfriend

to Eric Morecambe OBE and the Morecard will be yours.

Name..................................

Address..................................

Telephone number of your Own Girlfriend if between 18 & 25 ....

LESSON 1
Emerge dramatically from the Tunnel

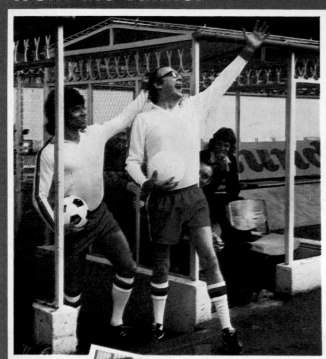

TIPS from the TOP

Kevin Keegan learns from the Maestro

Above: Eric in grand manner. Mike Channon looks on enviously.
Right: All wrong. Never be less than sensational.

LESSON 2
Make the most of an Injury

Left: Quite hopeless. Kevin wastes a golden opportunity.
Above: Eric in a life or death struggle.

LESSON 3 Whatever your feelings, don't show Dissent

Far Left: Graceful grovelling pleases the most hard-hearted ref.

Left: Kevin's little sign of displeasure will be noticed by the ref.

LESSON 4 Show affection to the Goalscorer

Below: A typical gesture lacking in imagination.

Right: 'My Hero.' Eric put warmth, feeling, romance into the celebration.

LESSON 5 Win a Psychological advantage at the Toss-up

The 'Tycoon Ploy.' Refuse to toss with notes of small denomination.

LESSON 6
Have your name taken with Good Grace

Below: When the ref asks your name, turning your back on him is impolite.
Far Left: Introduce yourself graciously and offer him your card.

LESSON 7
The Dummy

1 Eric, Wizard of Dribble
2 A quick shuffle of spectacles…
3 Kevin left helpless.

LESSON 8
Intimidate the Opposition

Right: Eric knows his worth.

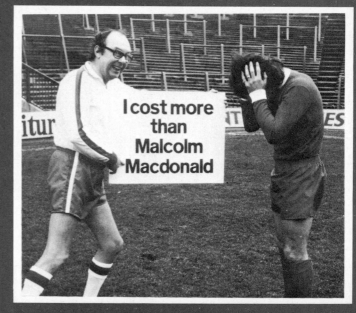

I cost more than Malcolm Macdonald

Don't appear to be the Aggressor

Left: If you are compelled to exercise a little force…
Above: Make sure to blame your victim.

Taking the Penalty

Below: The goalkeeper is alert, poised…
Bottom: Kevin introduces a substitute.
The goalkeeper remains alert, poised…

LESSON 11
Be a Crowd-Pleaser

Above: Eric shows Kevin a song and dance tactic.

Ernie's Plan

THE atmosphere inside Number 11 was grim. A taut, nervous Chancellor paced up and down, because the floor sloped. The Governor of the Bank of England, summoned at short notice from a secret address unknown even to his wife, slept uneasily on the sofa. In the corner stood the tall, sinister figure of a bespectacled Arab, tossing fivers casually into the open fire.

There was a knock at the door and a pretty secretary ushered in an even prettier visitor.

'Mr Wise to see you sir,' said Miss Tress softly, and departed, pursued by the tall bespectacled Arab. Wordlessly the Chancellor motioned the newcomer to a chair, switched off *Kojak* and took an old exercise book marked *Budget, half way through* from a drawer marked *Keep off Wedgie*. He passed it to the small distinguished stranger who scanned it rapidly, expertly, pausing only to ask the meaning of 'insolvent'.

· The Chancellor looked at him anxiously. 'What do you think of it so far?'

'Well Denis' (for it was he), said Ernie (for it was he), 'rubbish' (for it was).

The Chancellor burst into tears, grabbed a pre-packed suitcase labelled *Buenos Aires (please)* and made for the door.

'Not so fast young woman.' It was the voice of the tall bespectacled Arab who had returned unscripted and now stood arm in arm with the lovely Miss Tress blocking the exit. 'You forget that I, Sheik Yermoney, hold the keys and passports of the entire Cabinet, redeemable only on payment of the North Sea.'

'Moreover,' said Ernie, rising, though not very far, 'according to my rough calculations you owe the I.M.F. thirty billion pounds seven pee and Joe Coral six pounds fifty. My bill will be round in the morning with the heavies.'

The Chancellor collapsed like the pound. Then, he made a wild spring.

for Britain

'Don't go,' he cried, pinning Ernie to the floor. 'This is all your fault anyway.'

'All my fault Denis?' inquired Ernie, indignantly removing the pins and standing a little way up. 'Are you still beefing about my vast undisclosed and undeclared assets going on a numbered skiing holiday to Switzerland?'

'And look what it's done,' moaned the Chancellor. 'Everyone has left sterling, even the football team. Where's your love of old Albion? Have you no loyalty to Britain?'

'Nein.'

'No finer feelings?'

'I feel fine thanks.'

'No C.B.E.?'

There was a pause. Ernie, O.B.E., looked suddenly vulnerable; smaller; in fact almost invisible to the naked eye.

'You mean...?'

The Chancellor nodded.

'You won't go getting one for Eric?'

'You have my word as a friend of Harold Wilson'.

'Very well,' said Ernie, feeling with difficulty for his inside jacket pocket, for the movement was strange to him. 'How much do you want?'

'No little Ern,' whispered the Chancellor. 'It's not your money I want. It's your brain. Your rich, cash-intensive, liquid, surplus profitable brain. Tell me your secret,' he screamed suddenly, grasping Ernie by his shoulder pads and shaking him until the change rattled.

Ernie, visibly shaken, broke free and moved across the room to a grand piano where he composed himself.

'Alright Denis,' he said at length. 'I'll tell you.' He made a gesture. 'Since I was so low I have never in my life spent a penny.'

The Chancellor flushed. 'So,' he gasped. 'That's it. It's beautiful; classically, simply beautiful. We must do the same.'

'And quite by chance,' continued Ernie, 'I have brought with me a Master Plan.' So saying he produced from his trousers three new plays and a large piece of paper headed Master Plan.

He spread it on the floor. Then he scraped it off and the two men pored over it. The Governor of the Bank of England slept more soundly...

Ernie's Master

New Currency

A pleasure to have about the house; just as well because it can't be spent. Made entirely from soya beans, these luxurious notes and coins replace the boring old stuff. A national advertising campaign based on the slogan *You've never had it so what* will appear all over the place (which place to be decided). A new form of higher purchase will enable you to pay the highest prices without cluttering your home with what you've bought.

Fishing Limits

The 200-mile limit is to be rigorously enforced. British gunboats on wheels will patrol large areas of the Continent within these limits, and beyond if they get lost. By establishing a rightful claim to the banks of France, Switzerland and Germany, good fishing should be assured for years to come. Notes of small denomination will be thrown back until they get bigger. British housewives say they can get used to Swiss Francs and German Deutschmarks provided they taste like cod.

Sale of the Century

By answering a series of idiot questions you can buy a new antique for the price of an old one; a Life Assurance policy which expires when you do; and a selection of new releases from Pentonville. In addition you become eligible for Supplementary Benefits and get to grovel to Nicholas Parsons.

Sample Questions:

Easy for £1:
Would you like a cup of tea?
Is Bangkok a place or a nasty injury?
With one lump or two?

Medium for £3:
Name none of the Seven Wonders of the World.
Who wrote "Beethoven's Fifth"?
Who came fourth?

Impossible, for you!
Who said, and in what 19th or 20th century novel, "Yes"?
Who except a lunatic would want a shot in the arm?
Why is free collective bargaining so expensive?

Plan

Premium Bonds

Ernie the versatile computer switches to a new programme. By selecting losers only, the government saves a fortune. At the same time everyone has the satisfaction of getting picked each week. The scheme is not only fun, novel and exciting; it is also compulsory.

The Golders Green Tax Haven

In a recent questionnaire thousands of very rich people, asked what they liked most, answered 'money'. This wonder-scheme will bring them here in droves, enabling us to milk the Sheiks and to have Johann Cruyff and Franz Beckenbauer as foreign reserves.

Concorde to South America

Who needs to get to South America in a hurry? Who can afford to fly Concorde Anyway? Answer – the same people ! ! If you are an International Criminal bored with passports, baggage checks and customs, this unique service could be your ticket to freedom.

London's only Loo £100 a time

A mind-boggling device, making this a must for every tourist (average three times a day).

THE ERNIE WISE WALLET COLLECTION

IS THIS THE ERNEST WISE MK XX?

1 The Ernest Wise Mark XX; believed currently in use by the inventor but seldom seen; no recorded sighting since 1949.

2 Hand of the thief who tried to extricate the Mark XX from its inventor.

3 The 'Friends of Harold Wilson' Wallet; bears the slogan 'Peer Inside'.

4 The world famous 'I've lost my Wallet Wallet'. Unseen in pubs everywhere, it responds to the phrase 'my round I believe'.

5 The miniature Kamikaze Wallet (made in Japan). Commits suicide when opened.

6 Henry VIII's famous 'Alimony' Wallet, loved by his surviving wives.

7 The famous Ernest Wise Mark II, winner of the Interpol award for total security. Contents unknown.

8 The Windmill Wallet, launched during the Second World War with the slogan "We Never Open." Contents unknown.

9 The World Wildlife Wallet, prized by naturalists as the habitat of the only surviving family of Short Fat Hairy Moths.

THE WALLACE COLLECTION

...em pleased with my ...l plane takes me to ...ee Winston Churchill ...self as Head of German ...lain about my Russian ...ery nice and gives me ...He also offers me a place ...y does he want to shut ...of drawers? He tells me ...ar and am the greatest ...history. I say I must be ...ret to me. I become ...ntelligence.

...ss D-Day. I explain I ...have some people ...I am now Head of ...ish Intelligence and I ...y important. They ask ...France. I tell them not ...I learn a lot of details ...s of this particular trip ...ed about not being ...n Intelligence, I suggest ...er. I am made Head of ...ence, and I agree that ...except me) and the ...e) shall all go; and I ...n fight the Germans

...lost the war depending ...it. Churchill very pleased ...oin his Party. I ask if it is ...funny hats. I receive a ...elling me I am not Head ...nywhere anymore.

...an. What I need is a job ...n sure they will never ...out me.

What do you think of it so far?

THE WHITECHAPEL MURDERS

A Tale of Sheerluck Holmes and Dr. Witsend

"beyond even his remarkable capacities"

I still recall in every vivid detail that chill, cheerless, foggy November night in the year of '82, or perhaps it was '92. My friend and companion Sheerluck Holmes was seated directly in front of the fire in such a way that I was entirely unaffected by its warmth. He was smoking his evil-smelling pipe and playing on his violin a tune of such difficulty that it was beyond even his remarkable capacities.

"something regal about her appearance"

Our attention was arrested by the arrival of a tall dark handsome cab, followed by footsteps along our stairs and the unmistakable sound of a loud insistent knocking at our door.

"Ah," said Holmes, his keen senses directed at once to this singular chain of events, "unless my senses deceive me we have a visitor who is, I deduce, a woman of quality who is not used to being kept waiting."

"Holmes," I gasped, for his almost telepathic powers never ceased to amaze me, "this is amazing."

"Perfectly simple," said he, above the din, "for the point at which the hammering is located indicates either a man of improbably small stature or, as I prefer to speculate, a woman. Again, only a lady of quality cries 'we command you to let us in' in a high-pitched voice. As for her impatience," he cried triumphantly, "she has even as I speak grown tired of waiting and has gone away."

"Wonderful," I exclaimed.

When she called again I let her in and we found ourselves confronted by an elderly lady with, I thought, something regal about her appearance. Without a word she handed me the Crown of England she was wearing on her head, and I, courteous as ever, relieved her of her purple cloak and purse. Holmes examined her with his magnifying glass.

"Pray tell us your business," he said, "for beyond the fact that you are called Victoria, you are a Queen by occupation and if I play my cards right I could get a knighthood out of this, I can deduce little from your somewhat disappointing appearance."

"We were wondering if," she paused, "you do not object to our use of the Royal We?"

"It's first on the left down the corridor," said Holmes.

"You are quite a card, Mr. Holmes," she replied with a royal flush. "We were wondering if you had heard of a series of dread crimes called the Whitechapel murders and the name of one they call," she paused again, "Jock the Ripper."

Holmes played a dramatic chord on his violin. Then he rose to his full height, as he always did when he stood up.

"So, little Queen, you've come to confess to these heinous deeds."

Our visitor roared with laughter. "We are not amused," she said. "The point is that our dear son Bertie, one day to reign as Edward VII and, by the Grace of God, to be the subject of a T.V. series, is suspected of the crimes. Our faithful gillie John Brown is behind these rumours, the silly gillie."

"Holmes examined her with his magnifying glass"

"Witsend," cried Holmes, "write the good lady a prescription to calm her nerves. Take it to the dispensing chemist, gracious madame, and you will find it indispensable."

"You are a loyal subject," said she, "unmask the true culprit and you will earn a sovereign's thanks."

"And perhaps," smiled Holmes, kissing the ring upon her fingers, "a sovereign's hand?"

"Nothing doing," said she, kicking him on the shins, "I'm off." I handed her her crown and cloak, retaining the purse as a small souvenir of this momentous encounter.

"At least I've got the ring," said Holmes, hopping about in some pain as she closed the door. "And now we also must be gone, for somewhere in London's East End lurks a desperate criminal waiting to be brought to justice." "Tell me, Witsend," he said, putting on his heavy overcoat, "what do you know of this case?"

"hopping about in some pain"

"Holmes emerged from beneath the table"

"Only that a terrible fiend has murdered countless harmless souls, that he operates on foggy nights and that he leaves the bodies of his victims foully mutilated."

"I rather think," said Holmes, taking off his heavy overcoat, "that we shall stay in tonight."

At that precise moment there was another knock on the door. My intrepid friend bade me open it and took up a position under the table.

I was startled to find an odd figure before me, clad in a tartan kilt, a butcher's apron and holding in his hand a street map of Whitechapel.

Holmes emerged from beneath the table.

"I rather think, Witsend, I shall now go out."

"Hoots ye won't," said the stranger. "I have come to warn ye, for your own good, not to meddle in the affairs of," he paused, "Jock the Ripper."

Holmes thought deeply for two seconds flat.

"There is much in what this gentleman says, Witsend. I perceive that the murderer, whoever he may be, will stop at nothing, not even me. Honesty compels me to admit that I am simply not expendable."

"Excellent reasoning," I cried, "but what should we deduce from the bloodstained knife of the very type used to perpetrate the Whitechapel Murders which our visitor holds in his hand?"

"I had not overlooked that," said Holmes, contemptuously retiring behind the curtain. "Nor have I failed to observe the singular stains upon his sporran. I have made some study of the curious marks which appear on sporrans in London and have written a small monograph on the 347 varieties I have isolated. These are unmistakeably from Whitechapel and I have no hesitation in pronouncing our intruder none other than Jock the Ripper."

"You clever fiend," gasped our visitor, bolting into the street. I made to follow him, but Holmes, wiser than I, restrained me with a rugby tackle.

"Make haste Witsend," he said, holding me securely, "or the villain will escape. We must act with all speed."

We acted *Hamlet* as quickly as we could and were halfway through *Othello* when Holmes suddenly slumped to the sofa, to which he was addicted, and closed his eyes as he always did following some giant drain upon his intellectual resources.

"The villain has eluded my clutches, Witsend, and his identity we may never learn. But of this I am certain: his new-found respect for my powers will ensure that never again will he resume his dreadful operations, and of this I will inform our gracious sovereign in the morning."

"But what's this?" I cried, picking up a silver locket dropped by our visitor in his haste. "It is inscribed *To John Brown from We!*"

"Witsend," said Holmes curling his lip disdainfully and putting it in his pocket, "such a commonplace name is clearly an assumed one, cleverly adopted to conceal the Ripper's true identity. Useless as a clue, of course, but I perceive it may fetch a few bob in the Portobello Road."

"Holmes, wiser than I, restrained me with a rugby tackle.."

'We don't like people just because they're famous,' say Eric and Ernie, the People's Friends. 'They have to be rich as well.' This simple, homely philosophy has been their motto ever since, aged three, they caught a common cold. This so unnerved them that from then on they caught only the rarest and most exclusive viruses. Here are some of the illustrious characters who pop in and out of the Morecambe and Wise homestead to share a bag of crisps or a spin in the private sidecar.

Winning smiles for the Queen Mother.

A panic-stricken Napoleon with Vanessa Redgrave's Josephine.

With Richard Baker, the other newsreader.

Heart-throb Frank Finlay enchants Ernie.

Nina listens entranced as Eric sings

Ernie squares up to the formidable Oliver Reed.

A Statesman-like question from Lord George-Brown

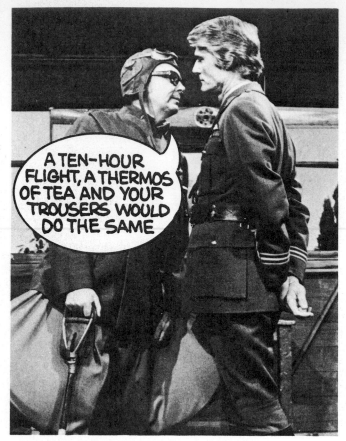

Pete Murray asks a silly question

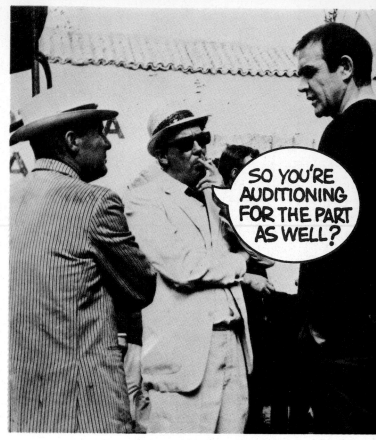

An encounter with Sean Connery, Mr Bond himself

With Andre Previn, alias Andre Preview

Opportunity knocks as Hughie Greene reads an Ern epic

A meeting of minds at the chimpanzees' tea party

THE VERY WONDERFUL JOKE PAGE

FAMOUS LAST WORDS

"Die my dear fellow?
That's the last thing I shall do."
Palmerston (we think)

"One of us will have to go."
Oscar Wilde (we think),
looking at repellent wallpaper

"This is no time to make new enemies."
Voltaire (we think),
asked by a priest if he rejected the Devil and all his Works.

"Aaaaaaaaaaaaaaaaaaaah"
General Custer (we think)

"I am dying beyond my means."
Mark Twain (we think)

"I'm sure I can take it with me."
Ernie Wise (we know)

The Italian War Joke

It's about the new Italian tank. It's got four gears. Three in reverse and one forward in case the enemy attacks from the rear...

FAREWELL TWO ARMS

The Hamlet Joke

Hamlet   *"Alas, poor Yorick, I knew him well."*

Horatio   *"He doesn't look a lot better now."*

THE GREATEST JOKE IN THE WORLD

There were two old men sat in deck chairs — One old man said, "It's nice out isn't it?— The other old man said, "Yes it is, I think I'll take mi

THE WORST PUNS IN THE WORLD

'I'm just not very tall,'
said Ernie, shortly.

'Three new plays to write this morning,'
said Ernie, playfully.

'Ernie, I'm going to break you in two little pieces,'
wisecracked Eric.

'I hate fishing,'
he carped.

'I've lost that new job,'
he said, disappointed.

'Don't let that bull near me again,'
said the matador, cowed.

'Anything in the Honours List?'
asked George, peering hopefully.

'Then I grabbed my parachute and jumped,'
he explained.

Join the dots

Eric and Ernie's CROSSWORD

ACROSS

1 If Lew invites you, you've made the . . . . . (5)
5 One of the famous short, fat hairy variety (3)
7 Oh Horror! For him you'll certainly have to pay (5)
8 Eric and Ernie's orders from the Palace (4)
9 An Ern play on the grand scale (4)
11 Like Ernie, a bit on the short side (6)
13 Oliver Twist's hungry request, or Eric without half his name (4)
14 Good-looking? Tall and dark anyway (8)
17 What actors do between engagements (and Eric's not averse to!) (4)
18 Eric's football team (5)
21 Could be tiny or big, but one of another pair of famous comedians (6)
23 Clever Billy to run a circus (5)
24 Those celebrated legs; short, . . . and hairy (3)
25 We thought she was just a newsreader till she discovered Morecambe and Wise (6)
26 Bring me . . . shine (3)

DOWN

2 What do you think of it so far? (7)
3 The singer Eric and Ernie most love to hate (3, 7)
4 All-knowing, just like Ernie (4)
6 The tall, good-looking one with the . . . . (7)
7 One like what Shakespeare and Ernie wrote (4)
10 Junctions – watched on television every night of the week (10)
12 Ray with the red breast (5)
15 Oscar Wilde recognized him as being important (6)
16 Famous actress who guest starred as Elizabeth I (6)
19 Sounds lordly but spells a great prize (6)
20 John, the singer pianist (5)
22 Can you see the join if Ernie wears one? (3)

3

4

2

1

♪ AND NOW

1. BRING ME SUNSHINE
IN YOUR SMILE
BRING ME LAUGHTER
ALL THE WHILE

2. IN THIS WORLD
WHERE WE LIVE
THERE SHOULD BE
MORE HAPPINESS

3. SO MUCH JOY
YOU CAN GIVE
TO EACH BRAND NEW
BRIGHT TOMORROW ♪ ♫

5

6

-THE SONG

MAKE ME HAPPY
THROUGH THE YEARS
NEVER BRING ME
ANY TEARS

LET YOUR ARMS
BE AS WARM
AS THE SUN
FROM UP ABOVE

BRING ME FUN
BRING ME SUN
BRING ME
LOVE

7

8

Eric Morecambe's SUN SIGNS

Aries

March 21–April 20

A bad year. Everyone you know is out to get you. Beware of strangers.

Cancer

June 22–July 23

You are ruled by Saturn, a miserable planet which will make rings around you. a good year for making a will.

Taurus

April 21–May 21

A fantastic time ahead, afoot, and in between for all tall handsome men in glasses called Eric Morecambe. Otherwise stay in bed, surrounded by next of kin.

Leo

July 24–August 23

Whatever you do, stay hidden. I foresee only gloom alarm and despondency for you. During the year you will gradually disintegrate and probably drop dead.

Gemini

May 22–June 21

Stark-naked horror looms. Blue-eyed blondes over the age of consent are advised to contact tall dark Tauruses named Eric Morecambe. They won't be safe but at least they'll go down fighting.

Virgo

August 24–September

You are ruled (out) by Jup rising and Mars falli Look out for a bright planet about to land on of you.

for the Coming Year

Libra

September 24–October 23

I foresee a spot of bother with plague. You will be troubled by boils, locusts and earthquakes. Your only consolation is that next year will be worse.

Capricorn

December 22–January 20

A wealthy film producer will offer you stardom in a disaster movie. Unfortunately the disaster will happen before filming begins. It's safe to fly, but not by aeroplane.

Scorpio

October 24–November 22

They say there's always somebody worse off than you. Not true.

Aquarius

January 21–February 19

A bright start to the year. You will catch fire. Don't feel put out; you won't be.

Sagittarius

November 23–December 21

You have an inferiority complex, stemming from total inferiority. Avoid appearances on *Mastermind*. If on *Sale of the Century* you will remain unsold.

Pisces

February 20–March 20

A bad year for Pisces and Incomes. You will have no money problems, no clothes either. You will suffer from recurring bouts of foot and mouth disease, impeachment, and, like everybody else, Nicholas Parsons.

Eric and Ernie

on holiday

The TITLER

Jennifer at the London Season

The Season got off to a splendid start with a long-awaited wedding. Lots and lots of important guests turned up, including the bridegroom. He was wearing a smart Moss Bros suit and seemed to be wearing rather badly.

Crufts was super! Doggy-people and people-doggies everywhere. Clement Freud, strengthened with extra thyamin, won first prize in the Parliamentary Whippet section. His owner, the unknown leader of the Liberal Party, earned a lucrative contract for feeding only on Wonderdog catfood for a year. 'Miaow', he barked a little later.

Perfect weather for Glyndbourne. How I loved the champagne on ice, the picnics on the lawns. I had a little of everybody's which added to the general fun, or at any rate mine. The evening was spoiled by some utterly horrid cabaret called, I think, Eel Traver-Tory, or some such person. Really! Next year I hope they let serious people get on with their own entertainment.

What fun at the Debs coming out! Lady Cynthia Havitt-Orf arrived with her debonair beau Claude St John de Vere Plantagenet Habsburg Bucket: Lady Gillian Tart-Crumpet was without her escort, fashionable man-about-town Ivor Profile who was somewhere out about town; in fact everybody who was anybody was there including Eddie Waring, who was up and under twenty times during the party.

The Queen was out in force to meet the English and West Indies teams at Lords. The sun shone brightly, obscured by heavy cloud and drizzle all day. Her Majesty asked Tony Grieg a technical question about his half-cock defensive prod and the ceremony was held up fully two seconds while he replied.

The Ascot Gold Cup was a glittering occasion. Lots and lots of important horses turned up. There was great excitement when the 100-1 outsider *Travel Dopefully* arrived in the Winners Enclosure because it came last.

The Garden Party at Buckingham Palace. How nice it was to be seen by so many notabilities. The Queen made lots of people feel at home by not asking them, so they stayed home.

Wimbledon was its usual self: strawberries, cream, and celebrities galore. There was tennis, too, and it was lovely to see all those athletic young men and women competing just for the sheer joy of the prize money.

The T.U.C. rally. Lots of pretty banners and simply *wonderful* placards. Also really *important* notabilities like Mr Hugh Scanlon (of the Shropshire Scanlons they tell me) and Mr Jones who apparently enjoys his social life so much he signed a contract for it with the Prime Minister, no less. How *nice* that there are still enough people with the leisure to put on parades like this instead of all being boring old working class.

Erica and Ernestine

Our wonder-girl reporter Angela managed to catch a glimpse of two ladies we don't often see up in Town. Erica and Ernestine are none other than twin sisters of the world-famous Eric and Ernie, respectively. "We don't often get out and about," they say, "because our brothers tell us we prefer a quiet life oop North in case we run into anyone they know in London." After meeting them Angela tells us she can see why.

How does it feel to be the sisters of the dynamic duo? "It feels lovely," they say, "all over." Do they see much of their brothers? "Ooh yes, we never miss them when they're on the telly." Do the boys send letters? "Lots and lots. Every time somebody sends them a letter they don't want they send it straight on to us."

They left their 10 roomed flat in Burslem at 4·0am in the morning to catch the January Sales at Harrods, London's most famous Department Store. "We know it's only October but we like to be early," smiles Ernestine.

Erica, quietly spoken and tall, adores buying gifts for her twin brother and Harrods is the only place for her. "I've managed to buy his birthday present already," she says softly, "but I can't tell you what it is in case he reads this," (a sudden girlish laugh). I asked them how it felt to be the sisters of such an admired twosome. "Oooh, great," they whisper. "We had a loovly dinner ("lunch" to you) in the Harrods Caf ("coffee shop" to you). We ate ourselves silly," says Erica. "But it were worth it!" giggles Ernestine. "Back to the diet tomorrow!"

My Greatest Speech

Delivered to the Lord's Taverners by the new President (that's me) in the presence of the retiring President, Prince Charles (that's him): Deafening applause, in which I joined.

by Eric Morecambe

Your Royal Highness... Mr President, that's me, Mr Chairman... that's him... Fellow Taverners... and you people here...

As this is my first speech as your President... I might as well warn you now... if you don't laugh... it won't be my last...

May I, Sir, welcome you on behalf of the Taverners to this luncheon. May I also say how enjoyable the meal was... the menu was superb. As a matter of fact I'm thinking of taking it to Timothy Whites and having it made up. Good lunches like this are like jockeys legs... few and far between.

As I look along this table I see people... some of whom I've known for almost an hour and a half. And I say to myself 'Ernie'...oh yes even I get mixed up... I say to myself 'what a fortunate man you are... how lucky you are'. Then I say 'why?'... and then I say... 'I'll tell you why sunshine'... then I say, 'go on then', and I say to myself... 'you are a fortunate man... because you have no enemies... no enemies at all... you have a lot of friends who dislike you... but no enemies...'

Any President wants his term of office to be a successful one... and also having had his Royal Highness as our last President, and having, in show business parlance, to follow that... makes me feel a little nervous... the last time I was as nervous as this was when I was trapped in a lift with Larry Grayson.

Having had Prince Charles as a President was a wonderful thing for the Taverners... and I'm not just saying that because you're here Sir... I'm saying it because I'm a crawler.

We were going to have a surprise for you at this luncheon Sir. We were going to cancel the whole thing and not tell you.

Also we were going to have a six-foot cake wheeled into the middle of the room... and a naked girl was going to pop out. But when we took the cake out of the oven she didn't look too good... so we've scrubbed around that.

I would also like you all to know that as your President I will not be a yes man... when the Chairman says no I'll say no.

I asked the Chairman the other day... 'how many people work for the Taverners?'... and he said 'about half of them.'

Later in the year I shall be going over to the States to have a word with my opposite number, President Carter. We should get on well together as we have a lot in common. He grows nuts and I am...

Ernie is thrilled at me being President, because, as you all know, Ernie has a great infection for the Taverners. He was going to be with us... but unfortunately this morning he met with a slight accident. He was cleaning Lew Grade's car when his tongue ran dry. But Ern is a nice man. At the moment he is doing government work.. he goes out with sailors (no disrespect Sir). Ern was in the navy during the war... he has a great war record, it's George Formby's. *I'm leaning on a lamp*...

Finally the war ended... Kaiser Bill was defeated so he came home. But back to realities.. so far as I'm concerned the idea of the Taverners is to make lots of money for our charities and at the same time to keep up the comradeship that exists in the Taverners. And to be able to make both money and friends through the game we all enjoy. Can't be bad...

I do realize that money is difficult to get at the moment... last year alone the cost of living shot up 30% a bottle. It shook Fred Rumsey... well, Fred likes a drink, and why not? He once held up a ship launching for three hours... wouldn't let go of the bottle. Anyway I digress...

I want my term of office to be as good, if not better than, any other President's... and with your help feel sure it will...

And now Sir; if I may ask you if you will accept from the Taverners a memento of your office and the time you have spent with us. This tankard, it's solid... solid what we don't know... but it has been inscribed with the Taverner's motto, Made in Hong Kong. It also has a list of girls' phone numbers from all over the world on the inside... the third one down's a knockout. If you ever ring that one and a man answers it'll be me.

On behalf of the Taverners may I be the first person this year to wish you a Merry Xmas and a Happy New Year.

Thank you Sir.

The Bank Robber
The famous Twopee

Madame Pompadour
The famous French cortisone

The Very last of the Mohicans
Me Red Indian Brave

The Pony Tail
I'm Ern—Ride Me

The photographic scoop of the year!

The Patriot
Britannia rules OK!

The Des O'Connor Fright Wig
Here comes King Song

Kojak
'Completely undetectable'-Columbo·

Superman
The natural look

GREETINGS FROM ERNIE

Emie

~~The Lord Chamberlain is~~

commanded by Her Majesty to invite

MRS WISE *and don't you forget*

to an Afternoon Party in the Garden of Buckingham Palace

on Thursday, the 13th July 1977, from 4 to 6 p.m.

Morning Dress or Uniform

Get Ill Soon

For YOU... and you alone

- ☐ Mrs Thatcher *
- ☐ Mary Whitehouse
- ☐ Fiona Richmond
- ☐ Basil Brush
- ☐ Danny la Rue
- ☐ Bionic Woman
- ☐ Angela Rippon
- ☐ Mrs Mao Tse-tung

Be my Valentine

* tick and pass on

Merry Christmas from Ernie

(You owe me £20)

POST CARD

Thursday, at the Bandstand.

Dear all at number 22, ~~10~~

We are having a ~~wonderful~~ holiday *Wall Street*
here at ~~Clacton~~. The weather is sunny,
champagne the sea warm and the food ~~quite~~ *very*
passable. The other people in the
guest house are ~~pleasant~~, *taller* we've met a
fairly ^ nice couple from Luton. Just going for
a walk on the prom so will close now.
Marcia
Regards to ~~Reg~~ and the kids.

Love ~~Babs~~
Ernie

TO: *All at Number 10*
(regards to next door)

London
W1

GREETINGS!
to my literary agent with 10% of my love

---

just
a little
reminder

24
SEPTEMBER

ERN'S BIRTHDAY

HAPPY

* Boxing Day!
  Christmas!
  Hallowe'en!
  Independence Day!
  Yom Kippur!
  Pancake Day!
  Orangeman's Day!
  Father's Day!
  Retirement!

from Ernie

* Delete where necessary

From Ernie with love xx

pst! Attach this card to your most expensive present

Ern's moving house

Ernie and Glenda

TOGETHER
IN

Last Tango in Harpenden

'Love means never having to say I'm off'

1. Love's Tender Awakening

Ernie, the handsome wealthy aristocrat, finds true love.

2. Declaration

Glenda declares herself; she has always longed for a man she can look up to.

3. The Orgy

A supreme moment of unbridled passion.

4. Proposal

Glenda tells Ernie of her prospects and proposes marriage.

5. The Bedroom Scene

Ernie creates a fuss over the phrase 'for richer or poorer' but nonetheless the wedding takes place at a fashionable Cash Registry Office. Afterwards, a searing, passionate climax.

6. The Volunteer

War is declared.
Ernie implores Glenda not to go.

7. Confession

Glenda admits all. She has deceived Ernie, is
penniless and can offer him only love.

8. The Duel

Realizing they can live together no longer, Ernie
issues a challenge.

9. The Incurable Illness Scene

Missing with both shots, Ernie hits on a better
scheme.

10. Reconciliation

A postman's knock, a letter, and Glenda has
inherited her long lost uncle's fortune.
All is forgiven.

11. The Happy Ending Scene

They lived happily ever after.

CONTOUR

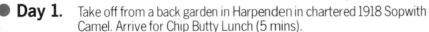

'7 Day Wonder' holiday—don't miss it!

No—<u>don't</u> miss this great offer of the Season! On the beautiful Costapakit. A holiday with a <u>difference</u>!

Your Super Itinerary

- **Day 1.** Take off from a back garden in Harpenden in chartered 1918 Sopwith Camel. Arrive for Chip Butty Lunch (5 mins).
- **Day 2.** Start work at 6.0am after typical British Breakfast (chip butty). First foundation to be dug before lunch.
- **Day 3.** Lunch—10 mins. Digging all afternoon. Evening: sleeping bags made up in first trenches. The joy of sleeping in your <u>own</u> trench!
- **Day 4.** Breakfast (Typical British). More digging. Lunch. First Scaffolding erected before tea. Resting period of 10 mins.
- **Day 5.** FREE—at least for the first 2 hours. Afterwards more scaffolding and girders. Roof on and spend night 6 in the hotel <u>you</u> helped to build.
- **Day 6.** Souvenirs on sale on site.
  Breakfast on return flight to Harpenden (Chip Butty). Rest.
- **Day 7.** Rest—FREE OF CHARGE.

*A subsidiary of M & W Holidays Ltd.

AN ARTISTS IMPRESSION

HOLIDAYMAKERS IMPRESSION OF THE ARTIST

Acknowledgements

Thanks are due to the many people who have made this book possible: in particular to ourselves, Glenda Jackson, Kevin Keegan, the Arsenal Football Club, the Duke of York Theatre, and to everyone whose picture appears.

A Star Book Published in 1978
by the Paperback Division of W.H. Allen & Co. Ltd.
A Howard and Wyndham Company   44 Hill Street, London W1X 8LB

First published in Great Britain by Weidenfeld & Nicolson Ltd., 1977

Copyright © Eric Morecambe and Ernest Wise, 1977

ISBN 0 352 30311 5

Art Director: John Rushton
Designed by John Rushton and Jacqueline Sinclair
Film Fun spreads by Denis Gifford
Illustrations by Jacqueline Sinclair, Rachel Beckingham, Helen Cowcher,
Steve Kingston, Neil Collins, Chris Woolmer, Gordon Cramp, Angelo Cinque.
Photography by Philip van Deurs, Behram Kapadia, Graham Brown. Stylist: Jane Crow Make-up: Rhian Meakin
Studio and photographic work: Cara Chase, Jo Harris, Focus Photoset, Geoff Goode Photographics, Dupes Associates.

Glenda Jackson was photographed at The Duke of York Theatre. The set was for 'A Bedful of Foreigners', designed by Terry Parsons; Glenda Jackson's dress by Harvey Nichols.

Photographs in the book are reproduced by kind permission of the following: Associated Newspapers Group Ltd (68-9); BBC (48-9, 50-1); Camera Press (photograph by Patrick Lichfield) (endpaper); Douglas Dickens (63, bottom right); Robert Estall (62, bottom right); George Greenwood (centre spread); Keystone (64-5, 2nd row left, 3rd row left); Popperfoto (6, 64-5, 2nd row right); Rex Features (18, 64-5, top row left and centre, 3rd row centre and right); Ronald Sheridan (62 top left, 63 top left); Sport and General (64-5, 1st row right, 2nd row centre). Photographs of banks on pages 64-5 are by kind permission of the National Westminster, Midland and Lloyds Banks.

Printed in Great Britain by Redwood Burn Limited, Trowbridge & Esher
Illustration reproduction by Radstock Reproductions

GOOD NEWS	**BAD NEWS**
Cheer up Eric, the news is that everybody's wages are catching up.	Yes, to mine.
An English team has just regained the World Cup.	True. It was led by Ronnie Biggs.
Fifty thousand people stopped smoking last year.	They dropped dead.
Wonderful! Somebody has just won half a million pounds on the Grand National.	Terrific. I'm the bookmaker.
Here's one from the Middle Ages. It says people are living longer.	Right. The Spanish Inquisition just installed their new rack.
Passengers on a Jumbo Jet heard the pilot announce slight engine trouble. Not to worry, he said it would be OK if a few of the crew bailed out to lighten the load.	It was a recording.
Racquel Welch wants you to watch the late night film on television with her.	I've already seen it.
Alright, here's bad news then. The Chinese have landed on the moon.	Not so bad. All of them.

THE AUTHORS

This dramatic photograph is one of the few first-class portraits of the internationally famous authors, Eric Morecambe and Ernest Wise. Winners of the Nobel Prize for Literature, the Pullitzer Prize and the Ernest Hemingway Memorial Trophy, they have dominated the Arts for many years. Their works include *Wars and Peace; Six Pillars of Wisdom; Two Cities, A Tale;* and *Hamlets.* Their originality has been a subject of controversy, but they are now widely regarded as unique.